Student Workbooks

Study Guide
Student Workbook for
I Will Always Write Back
How One Letter Changed Two Lives

By: David Lee

The Student Workbooks are designed to get students thinking critically about the text they read and provide a guided study format to facilitate in improved learning and retention. Teachers and Homeschool Instructors may use the activities included to improve student learning and organization.

Students will construct and identify the following areas of knowledge.

Character Identification

Events

Location

Vocabulary

Main Idea

Conflict

And more as appropriate to the text.

How to use this workbook

1. Complete as many entries as possible for each chapter.
2. Not all spaces need to be filled, move on when you have exhausted the information for the chapter.
3. Complete the Review page at the end to bring the information together.
4. Notes Pages and optional activities are located after the Chapter Pages. Use them to record any information not covered in the Chapter Pages.
5. Notes on the author can be kept on pages 4 and 5.

Author Notes

* Place any information about the author here.

Author Notes

Before Reading Questions

What is the reason for reading this book?

What do you already know about this book?

What, based on the cover, do you think this book is about?

Before Reading Questions

Have you read any other books by this author?

Is this book part of a series? If so what are the other books?

What are you looking forward to when reading this book?

* After Reading questions can be found in the back.

NAME:

TEACHER:

Date:

Chapters/Pages

* Not all number lines will have answers.

Characters
1.
2.
3.
4.
5.
6.

Locations
1.
2.

Conflicts / Problems
1.
2.
3.
4.

Events
1.
2.
3.
4.
5.

Possible Future Events
1.
2.

Key Terms / Vocabulary
1.
2.
3.
4.

Main Idea

NAME:

TEACHER:

Date:

Chapters/Pages

Events
1.
2.
3.
4.
5.

Not all number lines will have answers.

Characters
1.
2.
3.
4.
5.
6.

Possible Future Events
1.
2.

Key Terms / Vocabulary
1.
2.
3.
4.

Locations
1.
2.

Conflicts / Problems
1.
2.
3.
4.

Main Idea

NAME:

TEACHER:

Date:

Precognition Sheet (guess)

Who ?

What's going to happen?

What will be the result?

Who ?

What's going to happen?

What will be the result?

Who ?

What's going to happen?

What will be the result?

Who ?

What's going to happen?

What will be the result?

How many did you get correct?

NAME:

TEACHER:

Date:

Chapters/Pages

Events
1.
2.
3.
4.
5.

* Not all number lines will have answers.

Characters
1.
2.
3.
4.
5.
6.

Possible Future Events
1.
2.

Key Terms / Vocabulary
1.
2.
3.
4.

Locations
1.
2.

Conflicts / Problems
1.
2.
3.
4.

Main Idea

NAME:

TEACHER:

Date:

Chapters/Pages

Not all number lines will have answers.

Events
1.
2.
3.
4.
5.

Characters
1.
2.
3.
4.
5.
6.

Possible Future Events
1.
2.

Key Terms / Vocabulary
1.
2.
3.
4.

Locations
1.
2.

Conflicts / Problems
1.
2.
3.
4.

Main Idea

NAME:

TEACHER:

Date:

Chapters/Pages

Events
1.
2.
3.
4.
5.

* Not all number lines will have answers.

Characters
1.
2.
3.
4.
5.
6.

Possible Future Events
1.
2.

Key Terms / Vocabulary
1.
2.
3.
4.

Locations
1.
2.

Conflicts / Problems
1.
2.
3.
4.

Main Idea

NAME:

TEACHER:

Date:

Chapters/Pages

* Not all number lines will have answers.

Characters
1.
2.
3.
4.
5.
6.

Locations
1.
2.

Conflicts / Problems
1.
2.
3.
4.

Events
1.
2.
3.
4.
5.

Possible Future Events
1.
2.

Key Terms / Vocabulary
1.
2.
3.
4.

Main Idea

NAME:

TEACHER:

Date:

Chapters/Pages

Events
1.
2.
3.
4.
5.

Not all number lines will have answers.

Characters
1.
2.
3.
4.
5.
6.

Possible Future Events
1.
2.

Key Terms / Vocabulary
1.
2.
3.
4.

Locations
1.
2.

Conflicts / Problems
1.
2.
3.
4.

Main Idea

NAME:

TEACHER:

Date:

Chapters/Pages

Events
1.
2.
3.
4.
5.

Not all number lines will have answers.

Characters
1.
2.
3.
4.
5.
6.

Possible Future Events
1.
2.

Key Terms / Vocabulary
1.
2.
3.
4.

Locations
1.
2.

Conflicts / Problems
1.
2.
3.
4.

Main Idea

NAME:

TEACHER:

Date:

Chapters/Pages

Events
1.
2.
3.
4.
5.

* <u>Not all number lines will have answers.</u>

Characters
1.
2.
3.
4.
5.
6.

Possible Future Events
1.
2.

Key Terms / Vocabulary
1.
2.
3.
4.

Locations
1.
2.

Main Idea

Conflicts / Problems
1.
2.
3.
4.

NAME:

TEACHER:

Date:

Chapters/Pages

Events
1.
2.
3.
4.
5.

* <u>Not all number lines will have answers.</u>

Characters
1.
2.
3.
4.
5.
6.

Possible Future Events
1.
2.

Key Terms / Vocabulary
1.
2.
3.
4.

Locations
1.
2.

Conflicts / Problems
1.
2.
3.
4.

Main Idea

NAME:

TEACHER:

Date:

Chapters/Pages

Events
1.
2.
3.
4.
5.

* Not all number lines will have answers.

Characters
1.
2.
3.
4.
5.
6.

Possible Future Events
1.
2.

Key Terms / Vocabulary
1.
2.
3.
4.

Locations
1.
2.

Conflicts / Problems
1.
2.
3.
4.

Main Idea

NAME:

TEACHER:

Date:

Chapters/Pages

Events
1.
2.
3.
4.
5.

* Not all number lines will have answers.

Characters
1.
2.
3.
4.
5.
6.

Possible Future Events
1.
2.

Key Terms / Vocabulary
1.
2.
3.
4.

Locations
1.
2.

Conflicts / Problems
1.
2.
3.
4.

Main Idea

NAME:

TEACHER:

Date:

Chapters/Pages

Events
1.
2.
3.
4.
5.

* <u>Not all number lines will have answers.</u>

Characters
1.
2.
3.
4.
5.
6.

Possible Future Events
1.
2.

Key Terms / Vocabulary
1.
2.
3.
4.

Locations
1.
2.

Conflicts / Problems
1.
2.
3.
4.

Main Idea

NAME:

TEACHER:

Date:

Chapters/Pages

Events
1.
2.
3.
4.
5.

* <u>Not all number lines will have answers.</u>

Characters
1.
2.
3.
4.
5.
6.

Possible Future Events
1.
2.

Key Terms / Vocabulary
1.
2.
3.
4.

Locations
1.
2.

Conflicts / Problems
1.
2.
3.
4.

Main Idea

NAME:

TEACHER:

Date:

Chapters/Pages

Events
1.
2.
3.
4.
5.

* Not all number lines will have answers.

Characters
1.
2.
3.
4.
5.
6.

Possible Future Events
1.
2.

Key Terms / Vocabulary
1.
2.
3.
4.

Locations
1.
2.

Conflicts / Problems
1.
2.
3.
4.

Main Idea

NAME:

TEACHER:

Date:

Chapters/Pages

Events
1.
2.
3.
4.
5.

Not all number lines will have answers.

Characters
1.
2.
3.
4.
5.
6.

Possible Future Events
1.
2.

Key Terms / Vocabulary
1.
2.
3.
4.

Locations
1.
2.

Conflicts / Problems
1.
2.
3.
4.

Main Idea

NAME:

TEACHER:

Date:

Chapters/Pages

* <u>Not all number lines will have answers.</u>

Characters

1.
2.
3.
4.
5.
6.

Locations

1.
2.

Conflicts / Problems

1.
2.
3.
4.

Events

1.
2.
3.
4.
5.

Possible Future Events

1.
2.

Key Terms / Vocabulary

1.
2.
3.
4.

Main Idea

NAME:

TEACHER:

Date:

Chapters/Pages

* Not all number lines will have answers.

Characters
1.
2.
3.
4.
5.
6.

Locations
1.
2.

Conflicts / Problems
1.
2.
3.
4.

Events
1.
2.
3.
4.
5.

Possible Future Events
1.
2.

Key Terms / Vocabulary
1.
2.
3.
4.

Main Idea

NAME:

TEACHER:

Date:

Chapters/Pages

Not all number lines will have answers.

Characters
1.
2.
3.
4.
5.
6.

Locations
1.
2.

Conflicts / Problems
1.
2.
3.
4.

Events
1.
2.
3.
4.
5.

Possible Future Events
1.
2.

Key Terms / Vocabulary
1.
2.
3.
4.

Main Idea

NAME:

TEACHER:

Date:

Chapters/Pages

Events
1.
2.
3.
4.
5.

* Not all number lines will have answers.

Characters
1.
2.
3.
4.
5.
6.

Possible Future Events
1.
2.

Key Terms / Vocabulary
1.
2.
3.
4.

Locations
1.
2.

Conflicts / Problems
1.
2.
3.
4.

Main Idea

NAME:

TEACHER:

Date:

Chapters/Pages

Not all number lines will have answers.

Characters
1.
2.
3.
4.
5.
6.

Locations
1.
2.

Conflicts / Problems
1.
2.
3.
4.

Events
1.
2.
3.
4.
5.

Possible Future Events
1.
2.

Key Terms / Vocabulary
1.
2.
3.
4.

Main Idea

NAME:

TEACHER:

Date:

Chapters/Pages

* Not all number lines will have answers.

Characters
1.
2.
3.
4.
5.
6.

Events
1.
2.
3.
4.
5.

Possible Future Events
1.
2.

Key Terms / Vocabulary
1.
2.
3.
4.

Locations
1.
2.

Conflicts / Problems
1.
2.
3.
4.

Main Idea

NAME:

TEACHER:

Date:

Chapters/Pages

Not all number lines will have answers.

Characters
1.
2.
3.
4.
5.
6.

Locations
1.
2.

Conflicts / Problems
1.
2.
3.
4.

Events
1.
2.
3.
4.
5.

Possible Future Events
1.
2.

Key Terms / Vocabulary
1.
2.
3.
4.

Main Idea

NAME:

TEACHER:

Date:

Chapters/Pages

Events
1.
2.
3.
4.
5.

* Not all number lines will have answers.

Characters
1.
2.
3.
4.
5.
6.

Possible Future Events
1.
2.

Key Terms / Vocabulary
1.
2.
3.
4.

Locations
1.
2.

Conflicts / Problems
1.
2.
3.
4.

Main Idea

NAME:

TEACHER:

Date:

Chapters/Pages

* Not all number lines will have answers.

Characters
1.
2.
3.
4.
5.
6.

Locations
1.
2.

Conflicts / Problems
1.
2.
3.
4.

Events
1.
2.
3.
4.
5.

Possible Future Events
1.
2.

Key Terms / Vocabulary
1.
2.
3.
4.

Main Idea

NAME:

TEACHER:

Date:

Chapters/Pages

* Not all number lines will have answers.

Characters

1.
2.
3.
4.
5.
6.

Locations

1.
2.

Conflicts / Problems

1.
2.
3.
4.

Events

1.
2.
3.
4.
5.

Possible Future Events

1.
2.

Key Terms / Vocabulary

1.
2.
3.
4.

Main Idea

NAME:

TEACHER:

Date:

Chapters/Pages

* Not all number lines will have answers.

Characters
1.
2.
3.
4.
5.
6.

Locations
1.
2.

Conflicts / Problems
1.
2.
3.
4.

Events
1.
2.
3.
4.
5.

Possible Future Events
1.
2.

Key Terms / Vocabulary
1.
2.
3.
4.

Main Idea

NAME:

TEACHER:

Date:

Chapters/Pages

Events
1.
2.
3.
4.
5.

* <u>Not all number lines will have answers.</u>

Characters
1.
2.
3.
4.
5.
6.

Possible Future Events
1.
2.

Key Terms / Vocabulary
1.
2.
3.
4.

Locations
1.
2.

Conflicts / Problems
1.
2.
3.
4.

Main Idea

NAME:

TEACHER:

Date:

Chapters/Pages

Events
1.
2.
3.
4.
5.

Not all number lines will have answers.

Characters
1.
2.
3.
4.
5.
6.

Possible Future Events
1.
2.

Key Terms / Vocabulary
1.
2.
3.
4.

Locations
1.
2.

Conflicts / Problems
1.
2.
3.
4.

Main Idea

NAME:

TEACHER:

Date:

Chapters/Pages

Not all number lines will have answers.

Characters
1.
2.
3.
4.
5.
6.

Locations
1.
2.

Conflicts / Problems
1.
2.
3.
4.

Events
1.
2.
3.
4.
5.

Possible Future Events
1.
2.

Key Terms / Vocabulary
1.
2.
3.
4.

Main Idea

NAME:

TEACHER:

Date:

Chapters/Pages

Events
1.
2.
3.
4.
5.

Not all number lines will have answers.

Characters
1.
2.
3.
4.
5.
6.

Possible Future Events
1.
2.

Key Terms / Vocabulary
1.
2.
3.
4.

Locations
1.
2.

Conflicts / Problems
1.
2.
3.
4.

Main Idea

NAME:

TEACHER:

Date:

Chapters/Pages

Events
1.
2.
3.
4.
5.

* <u>Not all number lines will have answers.</u>

Characters
1.
2.
3.
4.
5.
6.

Possible Future Events
1.
2.

Key Terms / Vocabulary
1.
2.
3.
4.

Locations
1.
2.

Conflicts / Problems
1.
2.
3.
4.

Main Idea

NAME:

TEACHER:

Date:

Chapters/Pages

Not all number lines will have answers.

Characters
1.
2.
3.
4.
5.
6.

Locations
1.
2.

Conflicts / Problems
1.
2.
3.
4.

Events
1.
2.
3.
4.
5.

Possible Future Events
1.
2.

Key Terms / Vocabulary
1.
2.
3.
4.

Main Idea

NAME:

TEACHER:

Date:

Chapters/Pages

Events
1.
2.
3.
4.
5.

Not all number lines will have answers.

Characters
1.
2.
3.
4.
5.
6.

Possible Future Events
1.
2.

Key Terms / Vocabulary
1.
2.
3.
4.

Locations
1.
2.

Conflicts / Problems
1.
2.
3.
4.

Main Idea

NAME:

TEACHER:

Date:

Chapters/Pages

Not all number lines will have answers.

Characters
1.
2.
3.
4.
5.
6.

Locations
1.
2.

Conflicts / Problems
1.
2.
3.
4.

Events
1.
2.
3.
4.
5.

Possible Future Events
1.
2.

Key Terms / Vocabulary
1.
2.
3.
4.

Main Idea

NAME:

TEACHER:

Date:

Chapters/Pages

Events
1.
2.
3.
4.
5.

* Not all number lines will have answers.

Characters
1.
2.
3.
4.
5.
6.

Possible Future Events
1.
2.

Key Terms / Vocabulary
1.
2.
3.
4.

Locations
1.
2.

Conflicts / Problems
1.
2.
3.
4.

Main Idea

NAME:

TEACHER:

Date:

Chapters/Pages

Events
1.
2.
3.
4.
5.

Not all number lines will have answers.

Characters
1.
2.
3.
4.
5.
6.

Possible Future Events
1.
2.

Key Terms / Vocabulary
1.
2.
3.
4.

Locations
1.
2.

Conflicts / Problems
1.
2.
3.
4.

Main Idea

NAME:

TEACHER:

Date:

Chapters/Pages

* <u>Not all number lines will have answers.</u>

Events
1.
2.
3.
4.
5.

Characters
1.
2.
3.
4.
5.
6.

Possible Future Events
1.
2.

Key Terms / Vocabulary
1.
2.
3.
4.

Locations
1.
2.

Conflicts / Problems
1.
2.
3.
4.

Main Idea

NAME:

TEACHER:

Date:

Chapters/Pages

Not all number lines will have answers.

Characters
1.
2.
3.
4.
5.
6.

Locations
1.
2.

Conflicts / Problems
1.
2.
3.
4.

Events
1.
2.
3.
4.
5.

Possible Future Events
1.
2.

Key Terms / Vocabulary
1.
2.
3.
4.

Main Idea

NAME:

TEACHER:

Date:

Chapters/Pages

Not all number lines will have answers.

Characters
1.
2.
3.
4.
5.
6.

Locations
1.
2.

Conflicts / Problems
1.
2.
3.
4.

Events
1.
2.
3.
4.
5.

Possible Future Events
1.
2.

Key Terms / Vocabulary
1.
2.
3.
4.

Main Idea

NAME:

TEACHER:

Date:

Chapters/Pages

Events

1.
2.
3.
4.
5.

* Not all number lines will have answers.

Characters

1.
2.
3.
4.
5.
6.

Possible Future Events

1.
2.

Key Terms / Vocabulary

1.
2.
3.
4.

Locations

1.
2.

Conflicts / Problems

1.
2.
3.
4.

Main Idea

NAME:

TEACHER:

Date:

Chapters/Pages

* Not all number lines will have answers.

Events
1.
2.
3.
4.
5.

Characters
1.
2.
3.
4.
5.
6.

Possible Future Events
1.
2.

Key Terms / Vocabulary
1.
2.
3.
4.

Locations
1.
2.

Conflicts / Problems
1.
2.
3.
4.

Main Idea

NAME: TEACHER:

Date:

Chapters/Pages

Events
1.
2.
3.
4.
5.

Not all number lines will have answers.

Characters
1.
2.
3.
4.
5.
6.

Possible Future Events
1.
2.

Key Terms / Vocabulary
1.
2.
3.
4.

Locations
1.
2.

Conflicts / Problems
1.
2.
3.
4.

Main Idea

NAME:

TEACHER:

Date:

Chapters/Pages

Events
1.
2.
3.
4.
5.

Not all number lines will have answers.

Characters
1.
2.
3.
4.
5.
6.

Possible Future Events
1.
2.

Key Terms / Vocabulary
1.
2.
3.
4.

Locations
1.
2.

Conflicts / Problems
1.
2.
3.
4.

Main Idea

NAME:

TEACHER:

Date:

Chapters/Pages

Not all number lines will have answers.

Characters
1.
2.
3.
4.
5.
6.

Locations
1.
2.

Conflicts / Problems
1.
2.
3.
4.

Events
1.
2.
3.
4.
5.

Possible Future Events
1.
2.

Key Terms / Vocabulary
1.
2.
3.
4.

Main Idea

NAME:

TEACHER:

Date:

Chapters/Pages

Events
1.
2.
3.
4.
5.

* Not all number lines will have answers.

Characters
1.
2.
3.
4.
5.
6.

Possible Future Events
1.
2.

Key Terms / Vocabulary
1.
2.
3.
4.

Locations
1.
2.

Conflicts / Problems
1.
2.
3.
4.

Main Idea

NAME:

TEACHER:

Date:

Chapters/Pages

Events
1.
2.
3.
4.
5.

Not all number lines will have answers.

Characters
1.
2.
3.
4.
5.
6.

Possible Future Events
1.
2.

Key Terms / Vocabulary
1.
2.
3.
4.

Locations
1.
2.

Conflicts / Problems
1.
2.
3.
4.

Main Idea

NAME:

TEACHER:

Date:

Chapters/Pages

*Not all number lines will have answers.

Characters
1.
2.
3.
4.
5.
6.

Locations
1.
2.

Conflicts / Problems
1.
2.
3.
4.

Events
1.
2.
3.
4.
5.

Possible Future Events
1.
2.

Key Terms / Vocabulary
1.
2.
3.
4.

Main Idea

NAME:

TEACHER:

Date:

Chapters/Pages

Events
1.
2.
3.
4.
5.

* Not all number lines will have answers.

Characters
1.
2.
3.
4.
5.
6.

Possible Future Events
1.
2.

Key Terms / Vocabulary
1.
2.
3.
4.

Locations
1.
2.

Conflicts / Problems
1.
2.
3.
4.

Main Idea

NAME:

TEACHER:

Date:

Chapters/Pages

Events
1.
2.
3.
4.
5.

Not all number lines will have answers.

Characters
1.
2.
3.
4.
5.
6.

Possible Future Events
1.
2.

Key Terms / Vocabulary
1.
2.
3.
4.

Locations
1.
2.

Conflicts / Problems
1.
2.
3.
4.

Main Idea

NAME:

TEACHER:

Date:

Chapters/Pages

Events
1.
2.
3.
4.
5.

* <u>Not all number lines will have answers.</u>

Characters
1.
2.
3.
4.
5.
6.

Possible Future Events
1.
2.

Key Terms / Vocabulary
1.
2.
3.
4.

Locations
1.
2.

Conflicts / Problems
1.
2.
3.
4.

Main Idea

NAME:

TEACHER:

Date:

Chapters/Pages

Events
1.
2.
3.
4.
5.

Not all number lines will have answers.

Characters
1.
2.
3.
4.
5.
6.

Possible Future Events
1.
2.

Locations
1.
2.

Key Terms / Vocabulary
1.
2.
3.
4.

Conflicts / Problems
1.
2.
3.
4.

Main Idea

NAME:

TEACHER:

Date:

Chapters/Pages

Events
1.
2.
3.
4.
5.

Not all number lines will have answers.

Characters
1.
2.
3.
4.
5.
6.

Possible Future Events
1.
2.

Key Terms / Vocabulary
1.
2.
3.
4.

Locations
1.
2.

Conflicts / Problems
1.
2.
3.
4.

Main Idea

NAME:

TEACHER:

Date:

Chapters/Pages

Not all number lines will have answers.

Characters
1.
2.
3.
4.
5.
6.

Locations
1.
2.

Conflicts / Problems
1.
2.
3.
4.

Events
1.
2.
3.
4.
5.

Possible Future Events
1.
2.

Key Terms / Vocabulary
1.
2.
3.
4.

Main Idea

NAME:

TEACHER:

Date:

Chapters/Pages

Events
1.
2.
3.
4.
5.

Not all number lines will have answers.

Characters
1.
2.
3.
4.
5.
6.

Possible Future Events
1.
2.

Key Terms / Vocabulary
1.
2.
3.
4.

Locations
1.
2.

Conflicts / Problems
1.
2.
3.
4.

Main Idea

Before Reading Questions

What parts of the book were the most enjoyable?

Which characters were your favorite and why?

Write a summary of the book.

Before Reading Questions

What are the 5 most important events?

Write a review of the book.

What is likely to be a plot to the next book?

Draw an advertisement for the book

Character Sketch

Name

Draw a picture

Personality/ Distinguishing marks

Connections to other characters

Important Actions

Character Sketch

Name

Personality/ Distinguishing marks

Draw a picture

Connections to other characters

Important Actions

Character Sketch

Name

Personality/ Distinguishing marks

Draw a picture

Connections to other characters

Important Actions

Character Sketch

Name

Personality/ Distinguishing marks

Connections to other characters

Draw a picture

Important Actions

Character Sketch

Name

Personality/ Distinguishing marks

Draw a picture

Connections to other characters

Important Actions

Character Sketch

Name

Personality/ Distinguishing marks

Draw a picture

Connections to other characters

Important Actions

Character Sketch

Name

Personality/ Distinguishing marks

Draw a picture

Connections to other characters

Important Actions

Character Sketch

Name

Personality/ Distinguishing marks

Draw a picture

Connections to other characters

Important Actions

Character Sketch

Name

Personality/ Distinguishing marks

Draw a picture

Connections to other characters

Important Actions

Character Sketch

Name

Personality/ Distinguishing marks

Draw a picture

Connections to other characters

Important Actions

Character Sketch

Name

Personality/ Distinguishing marks

Draw a picture

Connections to other characters

Important Actions

Character Sketch

Name

Personality/ Distinguishing marks

Connections to other characters

Draw a picture

Important Actions

Character Sketch

Name

Personality/ Distinguishing marks

Draw a picture

Connections to other characters

Important Actions

Character Sketch

Name

Personality/ Distinguishing marks

Draw a picture

Connections to other characters

Important Actions

Character Sketch

Name

Personality/ Distinguishing marks

Draw a picture

Connections to other characters

Important Actions

Character Sketch

Name

Personality/ Distinguishing marks

Draw a picture

Connections to other characters

Important Actions

Character Sketch

Name

Personality/ Distinguishing marks

Draw a picture

Connections to other characters

Important Actions

Character Sketch

Name

Personality/ Distinguishing marks

Draw a picture

Connections to other characters

Important Actions

Character Sketch

Name

Personality/ Distinguishing marks

Draw a picture

Connections to other characters

Important Actions

Character Sketch

Name

Draw a picture

Personality/ Distinguishing marks

Connections to other characters

Important Actions

Character Sketch

Name

Personality/ Distinguishing marks

Draw a picture

Connections to other characters

Important Actions

Character Sketch

Name

Draw a picture

Personality/ Distinguishing marks

Connections to other characters

Important Actions

Character Sketch

Name

Personality/ Distinguishing marks

Draw a picture

Connections to other characters

Important Actions

Character Sketch

Name

Personality/ Distinguishing marks

Draw a picture

Connections to other characters

Important Actions

Character Sketch

Name

Personality/ Distinguishing marks

Draw a picture

Connections to other characters

Important Actions

Compare and Contrast Venn Diagram

Notes

Compare and Contrast Venn Diagram

Notes

NAME:

TEACHER:

Date:

Character Sketch

Name

Draw a picture

Personality/ Distinguishing marks

Connections to other characters

Important Actions

NAME:

TEACHER:

Date:

Comic Strip

NAME:

TEACHER:

Date:

Draw the Scene: What five things have you included in the scene?

1   2   3

4   5

NAME:

TEACHER:

Date:

Interview: Who _____

Question:

Answer:

Question:

Answer:

Question:

Answer:

Question:

Answer:

NAME:

TEACHER:

Date:

Lost Scene: Write a scene that takes place between _____ and _____

NAME:

TEACHER:

Date:

Making Connections

What is the connection?

NAME:

TEACHER:

Date:

Research connections

Source (URL, Book, Magazine, Interview)

What am I researching?

Facts I found that could be useful or notes

1.

2.

3.

4.

5.

6.

NAME:

TEACHER:

Date:

Sequencing or timeline

1.

2.

3.

4.

5.

NAME:

TEACHER:

Date:

Research connections

Source (URL, Book, Magazine, Interview)

What am I researching?

Facts I found that could be useful or notes

1.

2.

3.

4.

5.

6.

NAME:

TEACHER:

Date:

Sequencing or timeline

1.

2.

3.

4.

5.

NAME:

TEACHER:

Date:

Research connections

Source (URL, Book, Magazine, Interview)

What am I researching?

Facts I found that could be useful or notes

1.

2.

3.

4.

5.

6.

NAME:

TEACHER:

Date:

Sequencing or timeline

1.

2.

3.

4.

5.

NAME:

TEACHER:

Date:

Support This!

Supporting text

What page?

Supporting text

What page?

Central idea or statement

_____

Supporting text

What page?

Supporting text

What page?

NAME:

TEACHER:

Date:

Travel Brochure

Why should you visit?

What are you going to see?

Map

Special Events

Notes

NAME:

TEACHER:

Date:

* <u>Not all number lines will have answers.</u>

Main Characters
1.
2.
3.
4.
5.
6.
7.
8.
9.
10.
11.
12.
13.
14.
15.
16.
17.
18.

Important Locations
1.
2.
3.
4.
5.

Resolved Conflicts / Problems
1.
2.
3.
4.
5.
6.
7.
8.
9.
10.
11.
12.

Notes

NAME:

TEACHER:

Continued

Date:

Main Idea of the Novel

Most Important Events

1.
2.
3.
4.
5.
6.
7.
8.
9.
10.

Unresolved Conflicts / Problems

1.
2.
3.
4.
5.
6.
7.
8.
9.
10.
11.
12.

Possible Future Events

1.
2.
3.
4.
5.
6.

Made in the USA
Middletown, DE
20 December 2018